COMMUNITY FOUNDATIONS AS COMMUNITY LEADERS: A COMPREHENSIVE LITERATURE REVIEW AND FUTURE FRAMEWORK

Colton Strawser Consulting
Founded in 2012, Colton Strawser Consulting is a full-service consulting firm that empowers nonprofit organizations, foundations, and other groups seeking to change the world. Creating change can be hard, but with Colton Strawser Consulting it can be a little easier. Building upon years of service in the nonprofit sector, Colton C. Strawser, created Colton Strawser Consulting to assist organizations to create change by using practical experience and academic perspectives.

Community Leadership, Engagement, and Research Institute
The Community Leadership, Engagement, and Research (CLEAR) Institute is a nonprofit organization dedicated to bridging research and practice by conducting community-based research in order to empower communities with the data they need to create change.

Cite As
Strawser, C. (2021). *Community foundations as community leaders: A comprehensive literature review and future framework.* Arlington, Texas: Community Leadership, Engagement, and Research Institute.

Copyright © 2021. All Rights Reserved.

Colton Strawser Strategies, LLC
Arlington, Texas
www.coltonstrawser.com
hello@coltonstrawser.com

Acknowledgments
This research was supported by the Ford Foundation [Grant Number 135070].

Empowering Organizations to Create Change®

EXECUTIVE SUMMARY

Community foundations claim to play an integral role in fostering philanthropy at a community level all across the United States. Community foundations have three distinct operational roles, including asset building, grantmaking, and community leadership. While asset building and grantmaking have methods available to quantify and measure their impact, community leadership has remained an elusive concept for community foundations for many years.

This report shares the background on *community leadership,* as a concept, and covers the history of how community foundations have interpreted the role of community leadership over the years.

While critiques are made of current frameworks and historical approaches, it is all done in a good-faith effort in order to show how the community foundation field has collectively progressed, and what work still needs to be done for community foundations to fully embrace their community leadership role - and that role is going to look different for each community foundation.

The report includes a conceptual framework of community leadership based on existing studies and practical guidelines, including the use of civic leadership, collective leadership, and community engagement. The framework provides an opportunity to apply leadership at the institutional level and assists in examining nonprofit organizations as the unit of analysis, thus provide a more operationalized vision of community leadership.

COLTON C. STRAWSER, PH.D.

COMMUNITY FOUNDATIONS AS COMMUNITY LEADERS

Community foundations claim to play an integral role in fostering philanthropy at a community level all across the United States. Arguably the most identifiable form of community philanthropy (Sacks, 2014), community foundations are often the institutions sought after when it comes to mobilizing a community's resources to meet its needs (Mazany & Perry, 2014). In the 1990s, the Council on Foundations created a variety of tools and resources that explored the roles, responsibilities, and benefits of community foundations. One result of this effort to better specify the roles of community foundations was the introduction of "community leadership" as a new framework for the relations between a foundation and its community.

Community leadership is often the role most neglected when it comes to research on community foundations, yet it has the potential to be the most substantial role of the foundation. Community foundations can leverage their community knowledge, convening capabilities, and vast connections around particular issue areas to enact community-wide change. While remaining neutral on community issues was an option in the past, community foundations are now operating within a competitive market (Cantor, 2018; Ragey, Masaoka, & Peters, 2005); therefore, serving as a community leader can provide a competitive advantage in terms of fundraising, but can also catalyze groups and organizations to enact change by leaning into their role as a community leader.

The introduction of community leadership can be understood as a form of normative isomorphic pressure on community foundations. As the leading membership organization for community foundations in the United States at the time, the Council's actions provided essential guidance by including community leadership as an integral role in the community foundation operating model, and later including community leadership in the National Standards for US Community Foundations process. Since the Council shared this role in 1990 and later included it within its National Standards in 2000, one should expect that its membership adopts community leadership as a new norm.

However, it is unclear as to how many community foundations have adopted the community leadership role, and to what extent the community leadership role is a central element to the mission of community foundations. This report highlights the community foundation field's evolution in *community leadership* and provides an example of how community leadership can be approached operationally.

The concept of the community foundation was first conceived in 1914 by Frederick Goff, who was instrumental in creating the first community foundation, The Cleveland Foundation, and the concept then began to spread globally (Goff, 1919; Sacks, 2014; The Cleveland Trust Company, 1914). Community foundations are essential, local, philanthropic institutions that can help advance various issues and causes in communities to ensure all residents have a strong quality of life. Recent examples of community foundation work include advancing the United Nations' Sustainable Development Goals (Community Foundations of Canada, 2020; McGill, 2020; Ross, 2018), responding to COVID-19 (Sanford Institute, 2020; Soto et al., 2021), and taking on racial equity and power-sharing/shifting initiatives (Community Wealth Partners, 2020; Hodson & Pond, 2018).

Community foundations are often cited as playing three district roles within their communities: grantmakers, asset-builders (fundraisers), and community leaders. The practitioner and academic literature often expand on these roles (See Council of Michigan Foundations, 1992; Council on Foundations 1988; Philipp, 1999); however, within practice, these roles are often the various categories that community foundations use to segregate their work. To be considered a community foundation, all three roles must be at play, illustrated as a three-legged stool. Without executing each category in nearly equal measure, the stool may inadvertently lean to a specific role or may topple altogether.

Grantmaking   *Fundraising*

Community Leadership

Community foundations have claimed community leadership as part of the foundation operating model as early as the 1990s. In a Council on Foundations (1990) training manual for community foundations, the rationale for community foundations to take up leadership are that (1) community foundations are created to serve the community, (2) the board represents the community, (3) the community foundation is impartial in political matters, (4) leadership grows out of grantmaking since the community foundation is aware of community issues, and (5) unrestricted funds enable the community foundation to put resources to use for new and creative community solutions (p. 16).

CFLeads, a national network of community foundations committed to building stronger communities through community leadership, has developed various guides, assessments, and tools to assist community foundations in considering the community leadership role it plays. According to CFLeads (2008), community leadership looks like the following when it is enacted:

> **The community foundation is a catalyzing force that creates a better future for all by addressing the community's most critical or persistent challenges, inclusively uniting people, institutions and resources, and producing significant, widely shared and lasting results (p. 2).**

The above definition is focused on the outputs of implementing community leadership and neglects to mention the inputs, activities, or outcomes. In an updated framework for community leadership, the Council on Foundations and CFLeads (2009) stated that community foundations could act as community leaders for the following reasons: (1) Community foundations are nonpartisan, (2) Community foundations have wide-ranging relationships, (3) Community foundations have convening power, (4) Community foundations have flexible resources, (5) Community foundations can flex their jurisdiction and tools, and (6) Community foundations have staying power. These items are more in line with the current operating environment of community foundations; however, it should be noted that other types of community foundations (faith-based and identify-based) have been created over time since many community foundations were created, due to the nature of wealth, by white individuals and are often still governed by white individuals (BoardSource, 2018; Hamill Remaley, 2019)

While some research and practitioner reports examine the why behind community leadership, very few offer insights into how community foundations can truly be community leaders through various actions. Many of these reports are often single case studies and with no generalizable, or even broad, findings. Community leadership can be conceptualized in many different ways, which can sometimes translate into funding, advocacy, convening, or even capacity building. The community leadership role can be an important catalyst for community change. Additional research on this important role is necessary for the field of community foundations to grow and develop into their community leadership roles.

Community foundations are institutional forms of philanthropy designed to foster philanthropy at a local level (Mazany & Perry, 2014). The community foundation concept was first conceived in 1914 by Frederick Goff, who was instrumental in creating the first community foundation, The Cleveland Foundation, and the idea began to spread globally (Sacks, 2014). Created as an alternative to a trust company specifically designed to accept and manage charitable contributions (The Cleveland Trust Company, 1914), the community foundation model offered an alternative structure for individuals wishing to make a long-lasting impact in their communities. The strength of the community foundation model is its staying power and ability to provide "...practical, helpful assistance for the portion of the community which at the moment stands most in need of help" (as cited in Goff, 1919, p. 13). Historically, practitioner and academic literature has explored the grantmaking and fundraising (asset building) roles of community foundation, yet there has been a gap within the literature in regards to the role of community foundation as community leaders – including how they serve as community leaders, what it means to be a community leader, who decides the role of community relationship, and why being a community leader is an integral role to the mission of community foundations.

Additionally, the concept of community leadership has been explored throughout the academic literature; however, there appears to be no consensus on whether community leadership applies to single individuals ("Community Leader"), is a process for which to accomplish things within a community, a collective of individuals working together to create change (e.g., policy change, increase in quality of life), or simply the leadership that is found within a particular community. These challenges are explored throughout this literature review, and while there is a debate on the unit of analysis in community leadership, it is clear that there are themes that link the varying definitions and conceptions of what community leadership is, how it affects communities, and how it can be a resource for community change.

This literature review and conceptual framework examines various works of literature, both academic and practitioner, from a variety of disciplines and finds that regardless of the framing, community leadership includes the themes of collaboration, planning, and implementation—indicating that community leadership is not necessary a role, but a process in which organizations must continuously participate in to the point where it becomes an integral process that is institutionalized within the organization and becomes an approach to leadership rather than a single incident. As community foundations seek to deepen their engagement with their local communities, it is imperative that a definition of community leadership be developed that can easily be interpreted and implemented. Presently, many of the definitions of community leadership are rather ambiguous, and a change in definition is needed to recognize that community leadership is a collective process that should work towards a defined community goal, rather than an individual position.

While the broad definition of community leadership is likely to continue to be debated, the elements that make successful community leaders can be found within other definitions of leadership within the literature, including the concepts of civic leadership, collective leadership, and community engagement.

The following sections provide an overview of the purpose of community foundations and their expansion, both in terms of numbers and roles within communities, as well as conceptions of community leadership and how community foundations seek to fill this role. This report concludes with a conceptual framework for community leadership by a community foundation that incorporates the themes and findings from previous studies on community leadership.

The Council on Foundations (1988) defines a community foundation and its roles as the following:

> A community foundation is a publicly-supported philanthropic institution governed by a board of private citizens chosen to be representative of the public interest and for their knowledge of the community.
> Community foundations uniquely serve three publics: donors, the nonprofit sector, and the community as a whole. Individual community foundations may focus to some extent on one of these publics over the other two (leading to considerable diversity in the field) but by structure and by regulation the community foundation must always serve all three.
> Its purposes are to:
> 1. Professionally manage and distribute income, and portions of the principal when permitted, from donors' charitable gifts and bequests in a manner consistent with donors' specific and general interests;
> 2. Maintain and enhance the educational, social, cultural, health, and civic resources of the community, through the support of qualified nonprofit organizations, and;
> 3. Through the actions of board and staff, provide philanthropic leadership and help create and promote efforts among the citizens to improve the quality of life in the community.
>
> (p. 3)

More concretely, community foundations are often cited as playing three distinct roles within their communities: grantmaker, asset-builder (fundraiser), and community leader. The practitioner and academic literature often expand on these three roles (see Council of Michigan Foundations, 1992; Council on Foundations, 1988; Philipp, 1999) and these roles are often the categories that community foundations use to segregate their work.

Expansion of the Community Foundation Model

According to the Community Foundation Atlas (2014), there were approximately 1,900 community foundations worldwide in the mid-2010s, referred to internationally as "place-based foundations." These place-based foundations contribute billions in grants annually to the global economy, each serving an average of 185,000 individuals in a specific geographic region, with nearly two-thirds established over the past 30 years (Community Foundation Atlas, 2014).

Research focused on recounting and remapping community foundations in the United States suggests that over 1,000 community foundations serve approximately 98 percent of the country—geographically speaking (Wu, 2019; Wu, Paarlberg, Strawser, Ming, & Ai, 2019). These findings illustrate that what is often referred to as the "community foundation movement" is alive and well in the United States. As the community foundation field has evolved, so have the philanthropy support organizations (PSOs) that provide specialized services to community foundations such as CFLeads (Community Leadership), CFInsights (Data and Research), ProNet (Grantmaking), AdNet (Fundraising), and CommA (Communications), among others. This growth indicates substantial efforts toward professionalizing the field.

Conceptions of Community and the Role of Community Foundations

The word community evokes a multitude of meanings, especially in a globalized world. Hillary (1995) describes 94 different variations of community, indicating a broad spectrum of the concept's meaning. Wilkinson (1979, 1991) describes community as an interactional approach where community is built on the principle that the community acts as a whole within a social field and seeks to fulfill residents' needs. Milofsky's (2019) various definitions include individuals who share the same profession (e.g., nurses or teachers), seek emotional or spiritual connection (e.g., bible study or a church group), belong to a specific user community sharing a similar product or service (e.g., video games or a knitting circle), or elite groups of individuals (e.g., Nobel Prize winners or UN Ambassadors). McMillian and Chavis (1986) identify four dimensions that create a "sense of community": membership (feeling of belonging), influence (making a difference), reinforcement (fulfilled needs), and emotional connection (sharing strong bonds with others).

Sociologists often consider community to be bound within a geographic region, such as neighborhoods, towns, or counties (Fisher, 1994; Kasarda & Janowitz, 1974; Long, 1958; Sampson, 2012, 2015). While sociologists consider community to be a broad term with multiple dimensions (McMillan & Chavis, 1986), numerous studies define it geographically by examining various characteristics and disparities (Sampson, Morenoff, & Gannon-Rowley, 2002). For example, previous scholars have examined differentiation within communities on the topics of crime (Kling, Ludwig, & Kratz, 2005; Sampson, 1985), educational attainment (Garner & Raudenbush, 1991; Patacchini & Zenou, 2011), poverty (Harding, 2003; South & Crowder, 1999), and health (Larsen & Merlo, 2005; Leventhal & Brooks-Gunn, 2003).

Much of the literature on community leadership defines community in terms of geography, specifically focusing on neighborhoods or spaces of influence. In this literature, the extent to which an area is defined as a single community depends on the geographic composition of the area in question; for example, a rural community resident in the Midwest may consider community to exist at the county level, while a New York City resident may consider their associated community to be their neighborhood (e.g., Brooklyn, Manhattan, or Queens), or even special districts, such as Chelsea, Chinatown, or Greenwich Village. While other types of communities are explored in the social science literature, such as communities of faith, identity, and other attributes (see Franz, Skinner, & Murphy, 2018; McMillian & Chavis, 1986; Milofsky, 2019), the conceptualization of community within nonprofit and philanthropic studies is predominately geographical.

Following this line of thought, community foundations have historically defined community at the county level (Council on Foundations, 1990). In some cases, multiple community foundations serve a particular region of a county (e.g., San Diego Foundation, Rancho Santa Fe Foundation, Legacy Foundation, Del Mar Foundation, and San Marcos Community Foundation all in San Diego County, California), while others serve multiple counties (e.g., Central Valley Community Foundation serving Fresno, Kings, Tulare, Madera, Merced, and Mariposa Counties in California). Regardless of the particular geographic boundary, the standard definition of "community" for a community foundation is often place-based. However, other types of organizations use the title "community foundation" to create similarly structured organizations focusing on identity (e.g., Latino Community Foundation) or faith (e.g., Jewish Community Foundation or Catholic Community Foundation).

As part of their business model, community foundations claim to exercise leadership in their service area (Council on Foundations, 1988, 1990). While it appears community foundations have determined their operational definition of community (i.e., geographic), there is a lack of agreement on their definition of "leadership" and how they utilize leadership to achieve community-level outcomes—thus creating an operational challenge within the field resulting in having no normative clarity on how a community foundation is to pursue the community leadership role successfully.

Community foundations are unique organizations in their duality of roles (Harrow, Jung, & Phillips, 2016): they both raise and distribute funds. Additionally, community foundations are tasked with supporting nonprofits' needs while simultaneously fulfilling donors' instructions and wishes. Therefore, the operating model of community foundations is ideal if both the funding from philanthropists and the community's needs align. However, if funds are unavailable to support specific community needs, the community foundation can become stagnant and unable to address a particular need due to a lack of resources (Murphy, 2017). One possible way out of this dilemma is for community foundations to embrace and take on the role of community leadership.

Definitions of Community Leadership

"Community leadership is that which involves influence, power, and input into public decision-making over one or more spheres of activity."

Langone, 1992

"Developing community leadership begins with recognizing that both the practice of leadership and the situation in which it occurs need to be understood. We consider leadership as a collective relational phenomenon. This collective relational phenomena is also 'cultured,' that is, it is a phenomenon that grows out of, and is a product of its setting."

Kirk & Shutte, 2004, p. 235

"The pursuit of community wellbeing through strategic interventions that would not otherwise have happened."

Sullivan & Sweeting, 2005, p. 22

"Influenced largely by servant leadership (Greenleaf, 1977), community leadership is based on the notion that there are leaders everywhere, including civic groups, boards of volunteer agencies, neighborhood associations, interest groups, and self-help organizations (Tropman, 1997)."

Wituk, Ealey, Clark, Heiny, & Meissen, 2005, p. 90

"...community leadership emphasizes a collaborative, on-going, influential process based on the relationships between people."

Wituk, Ealey, Clark, Heiny, & Meissen, 2005, p. 90

"Community leadership, common to all community development projects, is the enabling of the relational capacity of community members to initiate the creative and often hidden potential of the community and turn it into initiatives driven by empowered community members."

Nel, 2018, p. 839

A majority of the definitions of community leadership emphasize concepts of collaboration, influence, long-term planning, advocacy, and mobilization as crucial characteristics of strong community leadership (Glidewell, Kelly, Bagby, & Dickerson, 1998; Langone & Rohs, 1995; Nel, 2018; Whitney & Trosten-Bloom, 2010). The emphases of definitions can be divided into those highlighting how such leadership emerges and those focused on what such leadership accomplishes. Based on the definitions listed on the previous page, community leadership is often collective – resulting in both voluntary associations and community institutions playing leadership roles within communities. Furthermore, the definitions indicate community leadership is about being active in pursuing change to achieve a civic outcome—whether the change be within the public policy arena, community development projects, or other initiatives affecting the life of the community.

Another essential element noted in the literature on community leadership is an argument that community leadership is not a style of leadership per se but may be more of a context in which leadership operates (Fanelli, 1956; Kirk & Shutte, 2004; Ricketts & Ladewig, 2008). For example, community leadership within the academic literature can theoretically refer to leaders within a community (person) or a place within a community where leadership is executed (e.g., an individual within a church, a principal within a school).

The community leadership literature's overall challenge is its focus on identifying leaders as individuals, a similar trend found in the literature in leadership studies. Yet, many of these community leadership studies lack an overall definition of what success looks like for a community leader and who decides who is a community leader.

Community Leadership vs. Leaders in Community

As previously mentioned, community leadership is complex and it has previously been conceptualized as a position, an action, an individual, a group, a group of groups, and other ways. In some instances, community leadership refers to individuals seeking to enhance the quality of life of a community. In others, it refers to leadership within a particular context (i.e., a "community"). While community leadership is not clearly defined within the literature, the various definitions of community leadership have some common themes—Working for the betterment of all and collaborating within and with the community—all of which have been more strategically explored within the academic and practitioner literature (e.g., community development, community engagement, participatory action research). Therefore, the conceptions of community leadership can be divided into two categories: (1) Community institutions seeking to create change within a community (i.e., externally focused) and (2) individuals that enhance their leadership skills to being competent leaders within community (i.e., internally focused)

In regard to the first category, community leadership requires action; therefore, community foundations can serve as community leaders in a variety of ways that seek to deliver on their overall goals and mission of enhancing the quality of life for a particular region. Leadership requires action (or inversely, inaction may be considered poor leadership); therefore, community foundations can serve as community leaders by engaging in public policy, serving as resources for information within communities, convening local organizations around a particular community issues, and a variety of other actions that seek to create a positive change within their service region.

While developing individuals' leadership skills within communities is vital, there is a difference between being a leader within a community and leading from within communities. There are many programs that seek to equip individuals within a community with leadership skills (i.e., individuals and internally focused) that can help them become more effective leaders within their personal and professional lives. Many community leadership programs focus on building skills needed for leadership (Galloway, 1997), which can be necessary to create strong community leaders, yet many of these programs are often focused on building individual capacity rather than increasing community or organizational capacity. For example, these types of programs aid individuals in understanding their leadership styles, instruct them on how to lead a team, and identify ways in which individuals can be more aware of their leadership traits to be a better leader (Galloway, 1997). What they fail to do is address leadership challenges within the community, indicating the community leadership programs are more about being leaders within a community, rather than leading a community forward by making a positive societal change.

Conceptual Definition of Community Leadership

As community foundations take on leadership roles to address some of society's toughest challenges, it is clear that a very specific type of leadership is needed. Based on a review of the literature and various theories related to the study of leadership and change management, the following is a working definition of community leadership:

Community foundations act as community leaders when they engage individuals or groups within a particular community to collectively establish goals and guide them toward the achievement of those goals to achieve a civic outcome.

As defined in this section, community leadership is a process that a community foundation can pursue to make positive changes in a community. Furthermore, community leadership is also a spectrum in which all leadership expressions may not look the same, yet the motivating principles are likely similar. For example, community foundations with limited capacity (i.e., few staff members, limited assets) may have a smaller leadership role in their community. In contrast, they could also be the primary institution driving change in the community if they are the only organization in the community providing strategic leadership. Thus, community leadership is very contextual. As community foundations seek to enhance their community leadership role, it is necessary to consider their leadership capacity, what they bring to the table, whom they need to involve, and collectively decide how they wish to move forward.

Community Foundations: Grantmaker to Community Leader

Although community foundations have existed since the early 1900s, the role of the foundation as community leadership was first introduced in the practitioner literature in the late 1980s and early 1990s (Council on Foundations, 1988, 1990). In a Council on Foundations (1990) training manual for community foundations, the rationale for community foundations to take up leadership within their communities were as follows: (1) community foundations are created to serve the community, (2) the board represents the community, (3) the community foundation is impartial in political matters, (4) leadership grows out of grantmaking since the community foundation is aware of community issues, and (5) unrestricted funds enable the community foundation to put resources to use for new and creative community solutions (p. 18).

A report from Community Foundations of Canada (1996) established nine community leadership principles that call for community leadership as an integral role within the community foundation business model and suggest such activities should be threaded throughout the operations of a community foundation.

Building Community Capacity - We will nurture and build our community's strengths and assets. Communities are strengthened by initiatives which increase the capacity of organizations and individuals to respond to challenges and opportunities, develop local leadership, promote self-reliance, emphasize prevention and mobilize civic participation and resources.

Understanding the Changing Nature of Our Communities - To be strategic in all our activities, we need to know our communities well. This involved spending time in community consultation, making ourselves available for discussion, being active participants in the community, monitoring local and national trends and being aware of the impact of change in our communities.

Creating Opportunities for Dialogue - Because of our broad mandate to nurture a vital community, we will bring together people with different ideas and points of view to create opportunities for respectful dialogue on issues of importance to our communities.

Developing Partnerships - Since more can be accomplished when acting together, we will form, encourage and support partnerships among individuals, neighbourhood and community groups, service clubs, foundations, professional advisors, businesses, governments, the media and others, based on shared vision and mutual responsibility.

Reflecting Diversity - We believe there is strength in diversity and that our communities will be better served when we understand different points of view and engage the broader community in our deliberations and decision making

Establishing an Effective and Imaginative Grants Program - We will strive to continually improve our skills as grantmakers, making a visible and lasting difference in our communities through a grant program that is balanced, flexible, creative and responsive.

Evaluating and Sharing Results - We will evaluate our activities to improve our skills and knowledge and we will share key findings with others.

Implementing Responsive and Accountable Processes - We will engage in practices that are open and accessible, fair and objective, flexible and timely with grant seekers, donors, volunteers and others in the community. This is essential to our role as credible and reputable stewards of community resources.

Balancing Our Resources - Because our fund development, grantmaking, and community leadership activities are interdependent, we will commit and balance our human and financial resources among them.

In a Council on Michigan Foundations and Council on Foundations (1999) training program for new community foundation trustees and staff, community leadership was described as a unique role for community foundations. The following training manual examples illustrate the rationale for community foundations to participate in leadership and convening:

- The community foundation is neutral – The Foundation's program and community advocacy activities are focus on community betterment.
- The community foundation is a bridge – The Foundation bridges the gap between the community of affluence and the community of need.
- The community foundation does not compete with other area organization in its fund raising activities.
- The community foundation has special insight – The Foundation's grantmaking position allows it to understand community / organizational capacity.
- The community foundation is isolated – Healthy isolation allows the Community Foundation to operate free of community "politics."

Bernholz et al. (2005) state that community leadership is an important tool for community foundations to succeed, and present three leadership tasks for community foundations, including shifting the organizational focus from the institution to the community, from managing financial assets to long-term leadership, and from competitive independence to coordinated impact (p. 35).

In 2008, CFLeads released its first iteration of the Framework for Community Leadership by a Community Foundation, with an updated version released in 2013 that acknowledged the potential community foundations had to lead within their local communities. According to CFLeads (2008), effective community leadership is the following:

> **The community foundation is a catalyzing force that creates a better future for all by addressing the community's most critical or persistent challenges, inclusively uniting people, institutions, and resources, and producing significant, widely shared, and lasting results (p. 2).**

With the creation of the CFLeads framework for community leadership, the Council on Foundations and CFLeads (2009) stated that community foundations are well-suited to act as community leaders as: (1) they are nonpartisan, (2) they have wide-ranging relationships, (3) they have convening power, (4) they have flexible resources, (5) they can flex their jurisdiction and tools, and (6) they have staying power. While these points are more congruent with community foundations' current operating environment, there is a lack of clarity on how community foundations become community leaders since the definition is primarily focused on the result—or "outcome."

Rationale for Community Leadership

Among the four rationales for community foundations to serve as community leaders listed above, there appears to be little agreement on the reasoning or approach for community leadership – other than many agreeing on the fact that community foundations are neutral and/or nonpartisan. There appears to be a slight adjustment in language over time that illustrates that community foundations may have become more aware of their power – changing rationales around their grantmaking being leadership and them being aware of community issues, to focusing more on convening and taking a community-centered approach to be more responsive to community issues. These alternations also appear within CFLeads most recently iteration of its community leadership framework and recently publications.

Council on Foundations (1990)	<ul><li>Serve the community</li><li>Board represents community</li><li>Impartial in political matters</li><li>Grantmaking is leadership</li><li>Aware of community issues</li><li>Unrestricted funds provide flexibility</li></ul>
Community Foundations of Canada (1996)	<ul><li>Building community capacity</li><li>Understanding the changing nature of our communities</li><li>Creating opportunities for dialogue</li><li>Developing partnerships</li><li>Reflecting diversity</li><li>Establishing an effective and imaginative grants program</li><li>Evaluating and sharing results</li><li>Implementing responsive and accountable processes</li><li>Balancing our resources</li></ul>
Council of Michigan Foundations (1999)	<ul><li>Community foundation is neutral</li><li>Focus on community betterment</li><li>Connects people with means to issues of need</li><li>Does not complete against other organizations for funding</li><li>Aware of community issues</li><li>Operates freely from politics</li></ul>
Council on Foundations and CFLeads (2009)	<ul><li>Community foundations are nonpartisan</li><li>Expansive relationships</li><li>Conveners</li><li>Flexible resources</li><li>Staying Power</li></ul>

Revised CFLeads Community Leadership Framework

In 2013, CFLeads issued a revised framework with an updated definition and outcome for community leadership by a community foundation that included language to frame the community foundation as more of a partner for bringing the community together with language that contains a more asset-based approach to leadership and community change:

> **The community foundation is a community partner that creates a better future for all by pursuing the community's greatest opportunities and addressing the most critical challenges, inclusively uniting people, institutions, and resources from throughout the community, and producing significant, widely shared, and lasting results (p. 2).**

In terms of defining community leadership's purpose or practice, the CFLeads definitions lack specificity in how community leadership can be measured and evaluated. The definition focuses on the "result" of implementing community leadership and neglects to mention the inputs, activities, outputs, or outcomes necessary to achieve the status of a community leader.

To assess how community foundations were approaching their community leadership roles, CF Insights and CFLeads (2017) conducted a national survey to identify community foundations' needs and future directions. The organizations reported five key service need areas: (1) staff development, (2) collaboration/networking and peer learning, (3) legal compliance and advisory services, (4) field positioning and leadership, and (5) field knowledge. Both CF Insights and CFLeads committed to creating metrics around community leadership, sharing information on critical community issues, and assisting other philanthropy service organizations (PSOs) that provide training and technical assistance.

As a result of the 2017 study conducted in collaboration with CFInsights, CFLeads (2019) issued five elements of effective community leadership that includes (1) engaging residents, (2) working across sectors, (commissioning and disseminating local data), (4) shaping public policy, and (5) marshalling resources. While these five competencies for the effective practice of community leadership help define what it means for a community foundation to be a community leader, the literature remains unclear as to how a community foundation would define or evaluate community leadership for themselves.

The CFInsights and CFLeads (2017) report alluded that leadership within community foundations did not quite have an evaluative component to it, which is challenging to establish when an overall definition is lacking both potential outputs and outcomes. Furthermore, the CFLeads framework lacks specific concepts that can be implemented. In contrast, other frameworks for leadership, organizational change, and community engagement such as Lewin's (1947) 3-Stage Change Model or Kotter's (1995) 8-Step Change Model provide both a specific definition for change as well as an evaluative component that assists in ensuring a particular goal is pursued. Those pursuing the goal are then held accountable for achieving the desired outcome.

In the CFLeads framework's (2013) current iteration, community foundations have the opportunity to classify what they do as community leadership if it fits within one of the five elements (engaging residents, working across sectors, commission and disseminating local data, shaping public policy, marshalling resources); however, there are no levels of effectiveness or impact that look at varying depths of engagement in community leadership. For example, two community foundations could state they are community leaders by indicating they strive to shape public policy. Community Foundation A meets with elected officials once a year to provide them with an update on the local nonprofit sector along with a copy of their annual report. Community Foundation B is part of three local coalitions working to increase affordable housing, advocates for additional funding from the state and federal government, and provides grant dollars to help support a housing index study to supply lawmakers with additional data. Both community foundations are engaging community leadership with public policy, yet Community Foundation B is clearly more involved than Community Foundation A, thus creating both an operative and evaluative dilemma for community leadership.

When foundations are left to create their own frameworks for success it can be somewhat arbitrary in the sense that foundations often hold the power in a grantmaking relationship, and thus the rationale behind conducting evaluations must come from a specific source to encourage performance measurement (Buteau et al., 2016). For example, initial rationalizations of community leadership by a community foundation focused on their power and connections to wealthy elites and ability to provide grants to support causes that were identified as important community issues. However, over time the rationale to be a community leader focused more on a community foundations ability to bring people together to focus on community challenges. Albeit an important shift in grantmaker power to implement more participatory practices, the community foundation field still appears to struggle with putting parameters around community leadership and identifying how it is implemented rather than what it looks like a result.

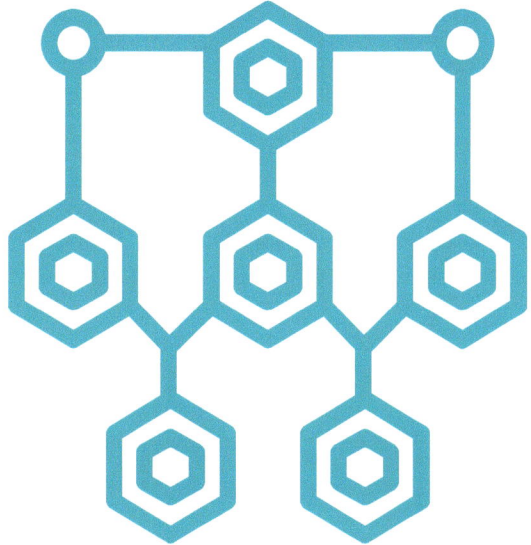

A Conceptual Model of Community Leadership

Contemporary community foundations are being forced to reconsider their value proposition in a time of increased competition from both for-profit companies (e.g., Fidelity, Vanguard, Schwab) and nonprofit entities (Ragey, Masaoka, & Peters, 2005) that offer lower-cost alternatives for philanthropic investments (Bernholz, Fulton, & Kasper, 2005). Community leadership is both the value-add and unique role that community foundations can play that provide benefit to both donors (e.g., knowledge about the community, ability to track local trends) and the community-at-large by leveraging their position in the community to raise awareness about various community issues (Bernholz et al., 2005; Council on Foundations, 1990; Canada Community Foundations, 1996).

Community foundations have an inherent responsibility to serve as community leaders since they are often the philanthropic powerhouses in a community (Council on Foundation, 1988, 1990). As institutions of philanthropy, community foundations have opportunities to convene conversations around particular issues within communities that are sometimes challenging for other nonprofits or entities in a community to address. While community foundations have been around for over 100 years, a majority of community foundations are approximately 30 years old (Sacks, 2014)—indicating that some community foundations may be farther along as community leaders than others. Leadership is often a response to a particular context; therefore, community leadership for community foundations will come in different shapes and sizes depending on their service region and other internal and external factors. Therefore, the choice for a community foundation is not whether they want to be a leader; it is a choice of how their leadership is expressed since it is part of their operational framework.

While the CFLeads (2008) framework on community leadership for community foundations is promising, it omits the various activities the literature provides as examples of community leadership such as how to convene different groups, strategies for collective impact, and other methods of participatory action within communities—causing there to be a gap in defining community leadership which prevents a standard for excellence in community leadership from being established. Upon extensive review of the literature, the theories of civic leadership and collective leadership, along with the act of community engagement, are likely the facets of community leadership that community foundations are often referring to in their practices. As the name implies, collective leadership is focused on achieving collectively defined goals that require collaboration, civic leadership is focused on making a difference in communities and enhancing the quality of life, and community engagement is an encompassing term describing how organizations are actively working within the community. The following subsections further describe civic leadership, collective leadership, and community engagement.

Civic Leadership. Civic leadership is focused on actions rather than positions or appointments (Couto, 2014; Kibbe Reed, 1996). Kibbe Reed (1996) argues followers can often be considered as leaders in their own right since they are part of the community where the leadership is executed and have agency as followers that authorize them to follow or not. Civic leadership is defined as activities focused on empowering others to contribute to the greater good of society. Historically, most community leadership programs focus on building the leadership

capacity of individuals for civic leadership: they are focused on fostering skills needed to lead and make change within communities (Azzam & Riggio, 2003). In order for such community leadership programs to be successful, "programs must come to understand leadership through collective action, where it is not confined to the individuals or established organizations" (Kibbe Reed, 1996, p. 103). Challenging the norms of traditional leadership, civic leadership is intentional, without position and power, and followers can often be the leaders (Couto, 2014). Couto (2014) argues that nonprofit organizations provide civic leadership in various ways, including offering cultural enrichment, social services, and other programs that seek to improve the human condition and the broader community. Couto's argument aligns with the definition of civic leadership developed by Kibbe Reed (1996):

> Civic Leadership is defined as the 'art and science' of leading in the public arena where one engaged in the affairs of society through public advocacy, debate, education, and the fostering of dialogue and group reflection. Civic leadership promotes critical thinking in the public arena and an examination of new alternatives and paradigms. Participatory leadership is promoted to enhance humanistic principles which prescribe and produce positive systemic change for the good of all society, including the world at large (p. 100).

While civic leadership is different from civic engagement, civic engagement could be the result or process of practicing civic leadership:

> Civic engagement means working to make a difference in the civic life of our communities and developing the combination of knowledge, skills, values and motivation to make that difference. It means promoting the quality of life in a community, through both political and non-political processes (Ehrlich, 2000, p. iv).

Collective Leadership. Sometimes referred to as shared leadership, the concept of collective leadership posits that leadership in groups is often a collective phenomenon (Contractor, DeChurch, Carson, Carter, & Keegan, 2012). As communities often come together to solve social issues, this framework notes that formal institutions that seek to help guide this change, such as nonprofit organizations, cannot single-handedly solve a social challenge. Compared to the more instrumental civic leadership concept, which focuses on accomplishing tasks and goals to create improvement, collective leadership is more expressive through its drive for inclusion and ensuring that everyone is heard.

The concept of collective impact, defined as a group of actors from different sectors gathering around a common agenda to solve a specific social problem, illustrates collective leadership in action. According to Kania and Kramer (2011), five conditions must be met for collective impact to move beyond simple forms of collaboration: (1) a common agenda, (2) shared measurement, (3) mutually reinforcing activities, (4) continuous communication, and (5) backbone support. As community foundations seek to lead in communities, they must recognize they cannot do it alone; it takes multiple stakeholders from all sectors to create social change (Kania & Kramer, 2011).

Community Engagement. In its simplest form, community engagement is focused on how community foundations engage with their community. Community engagement is often considered a physical presence within a community, yet this does not always transition to actionable leadership. Community foundations, and foundations in general, have been accused of focusing solely on the intentions of donors (Buchanan, 2017; Healy, 2018; Somerville, 2013); therefore, community foundations have intentionally sought to understand the challenges from a variety of stakeholder perspectives through various participatory methods (see, for example, Fund for Shared Insight ; Gibson, 2017, 2018). As community foundations are often viewed as knowledge hubs, they must be deeply embedded in various aspects of community conversations and initiatives (Council on Foundations, 1988, 1990). In the field of higher education, The Carnegie Foundation for the Advancement of Teaching's Elective Community Engagement Classification, (n.d.) which recognizes institutions of higher education for strong community engagement, provides a definition of community engagement that can also be applied to the work of community foundations: "Community engagement is shaped by relationships between those in the institution and those outside the institution that are grounded in the qualities of reciprocity, mutual respect, shared authority, and co-creation of goals and outcomes." As institutions consider becoming more engaged in their communities, they must be aware of power dynamics to ensure respect and reciprocity (National Center for Responsive Philanthropy, n.d.).

Leadership Approaches and Community Leadership

While leadership is often focused on the individual level (Burns, 2012; Heifetz & Linsky, 2017; Walumbwa, Lawler, & Avolio, 2007), many community institutions are collectively beginning to claim a leadership role to enhance the quality of life in their service regions, yet there is a gap within the literature on particular definitions and frameworks for institutional leadership. An example of this commitment is the work of anchor institutions, defined as place-based institutions, often nonprofits, that invest in capital and relationships within a defined area (Ehlenz, 2018; Webber & Karlstrom, 2009). According to Cantor, Englot, and Higgins (2013), anchor institutions are "...place-based organizations that persist in communities over generations, serving as social glue, economic engines, or both" (as cited on pg. 20). For example, many higher education institutions have adopted an anchor framework (Birch, Perry, & Taylor, 2013; Perry, Wiewel, & Menendez, 2009) dedicated to providing social, education, and economic investment in the community in which the university has a physical presence. Other institutions, such as hospitals (Norris & Howard, 2015; Reed, Göpfert, Wood, Allwood & Warburton, 2019), public libraries (Goodman, 2013; Mersand, Gasco-Hernandez, Udoh, & Gil-Garcia, 2019), and community foundations (Harrow, Jung, & Phillips, 2016; Kelly & Duncan, 2014; Mazany & Perry, 2014) have also been labeled as anchor institutions as their endowments ensure their staying power (Bowman, 2007, 2011).

The field of leadership studies has examined leadership from a variety of angles, including conceptualizing leadership as a process, as well as qualitative traits of individual leaders (Bass & Avolio, 1994; Cartwright, 1965; Lipman-Bluemen, 2005; Rost, 1991). Leadership theories can be valuable in considering how community foundations may seek to lead in an effort to create change within communities, yet there is an overall lack of empirical research on how nonprofit organizations serve, institutionally, as leaders in their communities. While this trend is understandable given that leadership theories predominately focus on one particular individual, a leader and followers, or a group of leaders and followers, nonprofit organizations play distinct leadership roles in communities that require further research and understanding.

Developing vs. Applying Community Leadership

Community leadership is not necessarily a theory of leadership – or at least it has not been applied and tested empirically enough to have a solid theoretical grounding. Yet, the act or desired outcome of community leadership can be found partially within existing leadership theories. While not present in the current academic literature, the act of being a community leader is most likely the amalgamation of multiple leadership theories and frameworks to creating systemic community change; thus, a single theory is likely unable to describe the leadership process of a community foundation seeking to improve the quality of life for a particular region.

While useful leadership theories address what it means to be a community leader individually, a majority of the research around community leadership analyzes community leadership programs (for example, see Keating, 2011; Langone, 1992; Langone & Rohs, 1995; Rohs, 1992). Community leadership programs have started for various reasons, including efforts to bring a community together, seek to fill leadership voids, and provide opportunities for individual leadership skill enhancement (Azzam & Riggio, 2003). Furthermore, many community leadership programs seek to serve a variety of individuals from the public, private, and nonprofit sectors. Thus, they may inadequately prepare individuals for community leadership positions (Langone & Rohs, 1995; Wituk, Ealey, Clark, Heiny, & Meissen, 2005).

Particular studies around leadership programs are often single case studies or involve examining one cohort's experience with a program on community leadership. While some studies indicate the overall "outcome" of participation in community leadership programming, there is a lack of evidence that completing a leadership program helps an individual become a strong community leader. Though some of these programs are focused on equipping individuals with leadership skills (i.e., having more leaders in the community), the literature remains unclear about how these programs help individuals create change within a community: leading the community rather than just being a "leader" in a community.

Community leadership programs are often focused on developing individuals' leadership capacity; while skill development is valuable, additional research is needed on community leadership in an applied setting. One way to pursue this line of research is to conceptualize community leadership as focused on building leadership in a community through skills-based development aimed at increasing individual leadership capacity—which is undoubtedly necessary to address leadership deficits and aid individuals in becoming better managers, more empathic supervisors, and understanding how other individuals work in a team environment. Another way to conceptualize community leadership is the application of leadership skills in order to improve the community (see Wituk et al., 2005).

Implementing Community Leadership

As community foundations seek to become more engaged in their communities and create change at a systemic level, there needs to be a reframing around what it means to be a community leader and how that leadership is evaluated (CFLeads & CF Insights, 2019). In responding to community needs, community foundations must be realistic about their organizational capacities to serve in the role of a community leader. Community foundations are unique in that they both raise and distribute funds, and community leadership provides an opportunity for community foundations to create a reason for individuals to donate towards specific initiatives in the community. Community foundations' fund minimums (i.e., $10,000 to create an endowment fund) may limit their engagement with all residents; therefore, community leadership is an opportunity to engage the entire community in collectively creating change. In practical terms, community leadership will look different for each community foundation; however, adopting a community leadership mindset and strategic positioning will allow community foundations to clearly define their value, raise their community profile, and create positive change within their service regions. According to a report from CFLeads (2020), 98-percent of surveyed community foundations indicated a desire to deeper or expand their community leadership over the next few years—signaling a potential wave of innovative approaches to community leadership and change.

Conclusions

Community leadership is important for any community to thrive, and community foundations are clearly in a unique position to provide leadership on a variety of issues within communities due to their access to funds and awareness of community issues. While community foundations claim the role of community leadership, there is still a lack of evidence on the process of being a community leader. Many organizations such as the Council on Foundations (1990) and CFLeads (2008, 2013) have provided a strong rationale for why community foundations should be community leaders, and CFLeads has shared what the result should look like, but the components necessary to be a strong and effective community leadership have often been excluded from the conversation. While community leadership will differ in various contexts, there must be some approaches or underlying strategy that community foundations can enact o be effective community leaders.

Many community foundations, likely find themselves at the tables where decisions are being made within communities, which raises questions regarding power dynamics, privilege, and position: Are institutions that are identified, or self-identified, as community leaders branded as such due to their wealth, power, and prominence—or are they rightfully seated at the table due to a proven history of community leadership? In an effort to bridge this gap within the literature, the definition used to guide this dissertation focuses in on civic leadership, collective leadership, and community engagement to build upon the idea that community leadership is a collective phenomenon that seeks to work with communities to create positive.

As community foundations consider their role as a community leader, it is crucial to fill various knowledge gaps to better understand the rationale behind engaging in community leadership activities. For proper assessment of community leadership to occur, additional research surrounding the definition of community leadership, both practical and aspirational, is necessary in order to measure it properly. As a definition is further developed, measurements can then be applied to the work of community leadership to ensure that community foundations are realizing intended outcomes for the community. Moreover, additional questions regarding who assesses the impact of community leadership (e.g., the community foundation, grant recipients, or community-at-large) will need to be explored as well. As the literature suggests. community leadership is one of the core operating activities of a community foundation; therefore, this dissertation seeks to understand how community foundations conceptualize their role as community leaders and pursue a community leadership agenda to enhance the quality of life in their communities.

References

Azzam, T., & Riggio, R. E. (2003). Community based civic leadership programs: A descriptive investigation. Journal of Leadership & Organizational Studies, 10(1), 55-67.

Bass, B. M., & Avolio, B. J. (1994). Transformational leadership and organizational culture. The International Journal of Public Administration, 17(3-4), 541-554.

Bernholz, L., Fulton, K., & Kasper, G. (2005). On the brink of new promise: The future of U.S. community foundations. San Francisco: Blueprint Research & Design Inc. and Monitor Institute.

Birch, E., Perry, D. C., & Taylor Jr, H. L. (2013). Universities as anchor institutions. Journal of Higher Education Outreach and Engagement, 7-16.

BoardSource. (2018). Foundation board leadership: A closer look at foundation board responses to Leading with Intent 2017.

Bowman, W. (2007). Managing endowment and other assets. Financing nonprofits: Putting theory into practice, 271-289.

Bowman, W. (2011). Financial capacity and sustainability of ordinary nonprofits. Nonprofit Management and Leadership, 22(1), 37-51.

Buchanan, P. (2017). Barbs, jabs, and the roles of community foundations. Center for Effective Philanthropy.

Burns, J. M. (2012). Leadership. Open Road Media.

Buteau, E., Glickman, J., Loh, C., Coffman, J. & Beer, T. (2016). Benchmarking foundation evaluation practices. Cambridge, MA: Center for Effective Philanthropy and Center for Evaluation Innovation.

Cantor, A. (2015). Strings from donor-advised funds are making supporters angry.

Cantor, N., Englot, P., & Higgins, M. (2013). Making the work of anchor institutions stick: Building coalitions and collective expertise. Journal of Higher Education Outreach and Engagement, 17(3), 17-46.

Carnegie Foundation for the Advancement of Teaching (n.d.). Defining community engagement.

Cartwright, D. (1965). Influence, leadership, control. Handbook of Organizations, 1-47.

CFLeads & CFInsights. (2017). Assessing community foundation needs and envisioning the future.

CFLeads. (2008). Framework for community leadership by a community foundation.

CFLeads. (2013). Framework for community leadership by a community foundation.

CFLeads. (2020). Going all in.

Community Foundation Atlas. (2014). Dimensions of the field: An in-depth analysis of the community foundation movement.

Community Foundations of Canada (2020). The Sustainable Development Goals and your community foundation - guidebook and toolkit.

Community Foundations of Canada. (1996). Principles of community leadership: A guide for community foundations. Ottawa, ON: Community Foundations of Canada.

Community Wealth Partners (2020). Moving toward equitable funding practices: Findings from research on community foundation practices. Washington, DC: Community Wealth Partners.

Contractor, N. S., DeChurch, L. A., Carson, J., Carter, D. R., & Keegan, B. (2012). The topology of collective leadership. The Leadership Quarterly, 23(6), 994-1011.

Council on Foundations & CFLeads (2009). Community leadership framework toolbox, Washington, DC: Council on Foundations.

Council on Foundations. (1988). A lexicon for community foundations. Washington, DC: Council on Foundations.

Council on Foundations. (1988). Community foundation competency guide: Self-assessment and action plan for professional development.

Council on Foundations. (1990). Community foundation training manual I: Mission.

Council on Michigan Foundations. (1992). Community foundation primer: An outline for discussion and initial organization start-up kit.

Couto, R. A. (2014). Civic leadership. The Oxford Handbook of Political Leadership, 347.

Ehlenz, M. M. (2018). Defining university anchor institution strategies: Comparing theory to practice. Planning Theory & Practice, 19(1), 74-92.

Ehrlich, T. (Ed.). (2000). Civic responsibility and higher education. Greenwood Publishing Group.

Fanelli, A. A. (1956). A typology of community leadership based on influence and interaction within the leader subsystem. Social Forces, 332-338.

Fisher, R. (1994). Let the people decide: Neighborhood organizing in America. Twayne Pub.

Franz, B. A., Skinner, D., & Murphy, J. W. (2018). Defining "community" in community health evaluation: perspectives from a sample of nonprofit Appalachian hospitals. American Journal of Evaluation, 39(2), 237-256.

Galloway, R. F. (1997). Community leadership programs: New implications for local leadership enhancement, economic development, and benefits for regional industries. Economic Development Review, 15(2), 6.

Garner, C. L., & Raudenbush, S. W. (1991). Neighborhood effects on educational attainment: A multilevel analysis. Sociology of Education, 251-262.

Gibson, C. (2017). Participatory Grantmaking: Has Its Time Come?. Ford Foundation.

Gibson, C. (2018). Deciding together: Shifting power and resources through participatory grantmaking. Grantcraft, Foundation Center.

Glidewell, J., Kelly, J., Bagby, M., & Dickerson, A. (1998). Community leadership: Theory and practice. Applications of Theory and Research on Groups to Social Issues, 61-86.

Goff, F.H. (1919). Community Trusts. Cleveland, OH: The Cleveland Trust Company

Goodman, E. P. (2013). Smart Cities Meet Anchor Institutions: The Case of Broadband and the Public Library. Fordham Urban Law Journal, 41, 1665-1694.

Hamill Remaley, M. (2019, July 12). A Long Way to Go: What Kind of Change is Needed Within Foundations to Advance Racial Equity? Inside Philanthropy.

Harding, D. J. (2003). Counterfactual models of neighborhood effects: The effect of neighborhood poverty on dropping out and teenage pregnancy. American Journal of Sociology, 109(3), 676-719.

Harrow, J., Jung, T., & Phillips, S. D. (2016). Community foundations: Agility in the duality of foundation and community. The Routledge companion to philanthropy, 308-321.

Healy, J. (2018). Philanthropy and leadership: Have community foundations lost sight of their north star?. StarTribune,

Heifetz, R., & Linsky, M. (2017). Leadership on the line, with a new preface: Staying alive through the dangers of change. Harvard Business Press.

Hodson, J. & Pond, A. (2018). How community philanthropy shifts power: What donors can do to help make that happen. New York, NY: Foundation Center.

Kania, J. & Kramer, M. (2011). Collective impact. Stanford Social Innovation Review.

Kasarda, J. D., & Janowitz, M. (1974). Community attachment in mass society. American Sociological Review, 328-339.

Kelly, M. & Duncan, V. (2014). A new anchor mission for a new century: Community foundations deploying all resources to build community wealth. Washington, DC: Democracy Collaborative.

Kibbe Reed, T. (1996). A new understanding of" followers" as leaders: emerging theory of civic leadership. Journal of Leadership Studies, 3(1), 95-104.

Kirk, P., & Shutte, A. M. (2004). Community leadership development. Community Development Journal, 39(3), 234-251.

Kling, J. R., Ludwig, J., & Katz, L. F. (2005). Neighborhood effects on crime for female and male youth: Evidence from a randomized housing voucher experiment. The Quarterly Journal of Economics, 120(1), 87-130.

Kotter, J. P. (1995). Leading change: Why transformation efforts fail. Boston, MA: Harvard Business School Press.

Langone, C. A. (1992). Building community leadership. Journal of Extension, 30(4), 23-25.

Langone, C. A., & Rohs, F. R. (1995). Community leadership development: Process and practice. Community Development, 26(2), 252-267.

Larsen, K., & Merlo, J. (2005). Appropriate assessment of neighborhood effects on individual health: integrating random and fixed effects in multilevel logistic regression. American Journal of Epidemiology, 161(1), 81-88.

Leventhal, T., & Brooks-Gunn, J. (2003). Moving to opportunity: an experimental study of neighborhood effects on mental health. American Journal of Public Health, 93(9), 1576-1582.

Lewin, K. (1947). Group decision and social change. Readings in Social Psychology, 3(1), 197-211.

Lipman-Blumen, J. (2005). Toxic leadership: When grand illusions masquerade as noble visions. Leader to Leader, 2005(36), 29.

Long, N. E. (1958). The local community as an ecology of games. American Journal of Sociology, 64(3), 251-261.

Mazany, T., & Perry, D. (Eds.). (2013). Here for good: Community foundations and the challenges of the 21st century. ME Sharpe.

McMillan, D. W., & Chavis, D. M. (1986). Sense of community: A definition and theory. Journal of Community Psychology, 14(1), 6-23.

Mersand, S., Gasco-Hernandez, M., Udoh, E., & Gil-Garcia, J. R. (2019, January). Public libraries as anchor institutions in smart communities: Current practices and future development. In Proceedings of the 52nd Hawaii International Conference on System Sciences.

Milofsky, C. (2019). Toward an Institutional Theory of Community and Community Associations: A Review. Voluntaristics Review, 4(1), 1-63.

Murphy, K. (2017). Community Foundation Business Model Disruption in the 21st Century. Washington, DC: Council on Foundations.

National Center for Responsive Philanthropy. (n.d.). Ignite the power of your philanthropy for equity and justice – Power Moves.

Nel, H. (2018). Community leadership: A comparison between asset-based community-led development (ABCD) and the traditional needs-based approach. Development Southern Africa, 35(6), 839-851.

Norris, T., & Howard, T. (2015). Can hospitals heal America's communities. Takoma Park (MD): The Democracy Collaborative.

Patacchini, E., & Zenou, Y. (2011). Neighborhood effects and parental involvement in the intergenerational transmission of education. Journal of Regional Science, 51(5), 987-1013.

Perry, D. C., Wiewel, W., & Menendez, C. (2009). The university's role in urban development: From enclave to anchor institution. Land Lines, 21(2), 2-7.

Philipp, A. (1999). Community foundations: Linking donors to communities. New Directions for Philanthropic Fundraising, 1999(23), 43-50.

Ragey, N., Masaoka, J., & Bell Peters, J. (2005). Convergence & competition: United Ways and community foundations – a national inquiry.

Reed, S., Göpfert, A., Wood, S., Allwood, S., & Warburton, W. (2019). Building healthier communities: the role of the NHS as an anchor institution. London The Health Foundation.

Ricketts, K. G., & Ladewig, H. (2008). A path analysis of community leadership within viable rural communities in Florida. Leadership, 4(2), 137-157.

Rost, J. C. (1991). Leadership for the twenty-first century. Greenwood Publishing Group.

Sacks, E. (2014). The growing importance of community foundations. Indianapolis, IN: Indiana University Lilly Family School of Philanthropy.

Sampson, R. J. (1985). Neighborhood and crime: The structural determinants of personal victimization. Journal of Research in Crime and Delinquency, 22(1), 7-40.

Sampson, R. J. (2012). Great American city: Chicago and the enduring neighborhood effect. University of Chicago Press.

Sampson, R. J., Morenoff, J. D., & Gannon-Rowley, T. (2002). Assessing "neighborhood effects": Social processes and new directions in research. Annual Review of Sociology, 28(1), 443-478.

Sanford Institute of Philanthropy (2020). Centering community in a pandemic: the impact of COVID-19 on East Bay nonprofits and the community they serve. Sanford Institute of Philanthropy at John F. Kennedy University.

Somerville, B. (2013). Keeping the "community" in community foundations. Stanford Social Innovation Review.

Soto, G., Supriya, K., Mika, G., Coffman, S., Saronson, B., Grabois, A., Ross, M., Neiheisel, K., Henry-Salami, N., Colar, A., Griñó, L., Webster, R., Gulliver-Garcia, T., Moore, K., & Entcheva, R. (2021). Philanthropy and COVID-19: Measuring one year of giving. Candid and The Center for Disaster Philanthropy.

South, S. J., & Crowder, K. D. (1999). Neighborhood effects on family formation: Concentrated poverty and beyond. American Sociological Review, 113-132.

Sullivan, H., & Sweeting, D. (2005). Meta-evaluation of the local government modernisation agenda: Progress report on community leadership and local government.

The Cleveland Trust Company. (1914). The Cleveland Foundation – A community trust. Cleveland, OH.

Walumbwa, F. O., Lawler, J. J., & Avolio, B. J. (2007). Leadership, individual differences, and work‐related attitudes: A cross‐culture investigation. Applied Psychology, 56(2), 212-230.

Webber, H. S., & Karlstrom, M. (2009). Why Community Investment Is Good for Nonprofit Anchor Institutions: Understanding Costs, Benefits, and the Range of Strategic Options. Chapin Hall at the University of Chicago.

Whitney, D. K., Trosten-Bloom, A., & Rader, K. (2010). Appreciative leadership: Focus on what works to drive winning performance and build a thriving organization. New York, NY: McGraw-Hill.

Wilkinson, K. P. (1979). Social wellbeing and community. Community Development, 10(1), 5-16.

Wilkinson, K. P. (1991). The community in rural America (No. 95). Greenwood Publishing Group.

Wituk, S., Ealey, S., Clark, M. J., Heiny, P., & Meissen, G. (2005). Community development through community leadership programs: Insights from a statewide community leadership initiative. Community Development, 36(2), 89-101.

Looking for a reference?

Many of the journal articles and resources included within this report may be out of print or difficult to access independently. If you would like to receive a copy of one of the referenced items in this report, please feel free to e-mail hello@coltonstrawser.com indicating which item(s) you would like by providing the reference.

www.ingramcontent.com/pod-product-compliance
Lightning Source LLC
Chambersburg PA
CBHW040056250526
45473CB00043B/1765